SPELLING

YEAR 6

PASCAL PRESS

Reading Eggspress Spelling Workbook – Year 6

Reprinted 2016, 2021, 2023

ISBN: 978-1-74215-311-7

Distrbuted by:
Pascal Press
PO Box 250
Glebe NSW 2037

Ph: (02) 9198 1748

Website: www.pascalpress.com.au

Publisher: Katy Pike
Series editor: Amy Russo
Editors: Laura Anderson, Stacey Belgre
Designed and typeset by The Modern Art Production Group
Printed in China by 1010 Printing International Ltd.

CONTENTS

WHAT IS READING EGGSPRESS?

Reading Eggspress is an online program designed to build language and literacy skills for students in Years 1 – 6. The program has targeted lesson sequences for Comprehension, Spelling, Grammar and Punctuation that align with national curriculum standards for achievement. With built-in rewards, access to over 2000 e-books and rich assessment data to track progress, the Reading Eggspress program individualises learning to help students achieve their personal best.

How does the Reading Eggspress Spelling Program work?

Research proves that students have more spelling success if they learn to recognise common spelling patterns and generalisations as part of an explicit and systematic teaching program. The *Reading Eggspress Spelling program* focuses on common spelling rules, generalisations and strategies using a combination of teaching videos, engaging online activities, games and tests with fully integrated student books.

The *Reading Eggspress Spelling books* for Years 1 – 6 extend students as they learn, use and apply their spelling skills across a range of written activities. The student books work alongside the online program to reinforce learning for each lesson.

The *Reading Eggspress Spelling program* is structured to provide instruction on a spelling rule, strategy or generalisation with 36 lessons per year level. Each lesson is centred on a carefully crafted word list, based around the sound, structure or meaning features of words. These word lists have been created by consulting educational research and the Australian Curriculum.

Self-paced systematic program

Easy to understand videos

Assessment and instant feedback

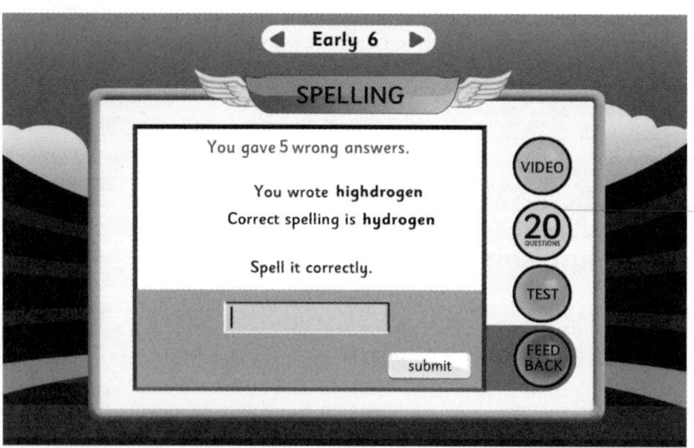

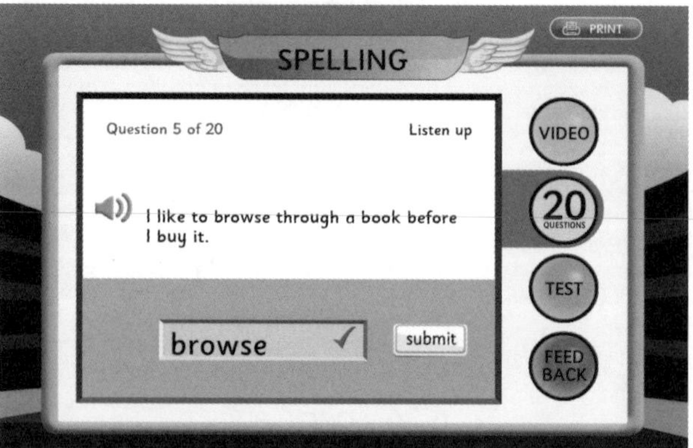

Practice activities

Spelling and the Australian Curriculum

Each lesson focuses on a core set of 20 words and 10 challenge words. These lists align with the Australian Curriculum Content Descriptions.

Literacy

Phonic and word knowledge

- use phonic knowledge of common and less common grapheme–phoneme relationships to read and write increasingly complex words (AC9E6LY08)
- use knowledge of known words, word origins including some Latin and Greek roots, base words, prefixes, suffixes, letter patterns and spelling generalisations to spell new words including technical words (AC9E6LY09)

Reading Eggspress Spelling

Each lesson uses a combination of activities from the following categories:

Proofreading: self-directed checking of written text. Proofreading assists the development of reading and writing.

Visual memory: the Look-say-cover-write-check creates a visual memory of the word. It is important as a self-correction skill.

Definitions: morphemic understanding of words. This skill is used selectively where an understanding of the etymology and morphological structure benefits orthographic understanding.

Word families: groups of words that share common morphemes. Identifying visual and morphemic commonalities aids accurate spelling and is used throughout the program.

Word sorts: groups of words that share a common theme. Word sorts have been integrated as grouping together like ideas helps learners make sense of the world around them.

Overview of Spelling Aspects Covered in Year 6

Spelling Aspect	Areas Covered	Pages
Digraphs and trigraphs	ea, ee; ai, ay; ie, ei; oa, ow	2, 3, 20, 21, 30, 31, 38, 39
Endings	ant, ent; ary, ery, ory	8, 9, 66, 67
Prefixes	un, mis, dis; re, de, pre; in, im, ir, il	18, 19, 42, 43, 70, 71
Suffixes	er, est; s, es; er, or; ful, less; ic; able, ible; ous; ance, ence; ness; ion, ian; ly; ity; ably, ibly; ancy, ency	6, 7, 10, 11, 12, 13, 16, 17, 24, 25, 32, 33, 36, 37, 44, 45, 50, 51, 54, 55, 60, 61, 62, 63, 64, 65, 68, 69, 72, 73
Letter patterns	igh, eigh, aigh; cc, xc	34, 35, 46, 47
Origins	Greek	40, 41
Other aspects of spelling	homophones; vowels; word building; compound words; loan words; tricky words; irregular plurals; eponyms; vowel exceptions	4, 5, 14, 15, 22, 23, 26, 27, 28, 29, 48, 49, 52, 53, 56, 57, 58, 59

MY PROGRESS CHART • LESSONS 6.1 – 6.18

Name ______________________________

Lesson	Level	Online test score	Pages	Self-assessment *With this list I feel ...*
6.1 ea and ee		/10	2 - 3	
6.2 Homophones		/10	4 - 5	
6.3 er, est		/10	6 - 7	
6.4 Endings: ant, ent		/10	8 - 9	
6.5 Plurals		/10	10 - 11	
6.6 Suffixes: er, or		/10	12 - 13	
6.7 Vowels		/10	14 - 15	
6.8 Suffixes: ful, less		/10	16 - 17	
6.9 un, mis, dis		/10	18 - 19	
6.10 ai and ay		/10	20 - 21	
6.11 Word building		/10	22 - 23	
6.12 Suffix: ic		/10	24 - 25	
6.13 Compound words		/10	26 - 27	
6.14 Loan words		/10	28 - 29	
6.15 ie and ei		/10	30 - 31	
6.16 able, ible		/10	32 - 33	
6.17 igh, eigh, aigh		/10	34 - 35	
6.18 Suffix: ous		/10	36 - 37	

MY PROGRESS CHART • LESSONS 6.19 – 6.36

Name ____________________

Lesson	Level	Online test score	Pages	Self-assessment *With this list I feel ...*
6.19 oa and ow		/10	38 - 39	
6.20 Greek origins		/10	40 - 41	
6.21 re, de, pre		/10	42 - 43	
6.22 ance, ence		/10	44 - 45	
6.23 cc, xc		/10	46 - 47	
6.24 Tricky words		/10	48 - 49	
6.25 Suffix: ness		/10	50 - 51	
6.26 Irregular plurals		/10	52 - 53	
6.27 ion, ian		/10	54 - 55	
6.28 Eponyms		/10	56 - 57	
6.29 Vowel exceptions		/10	58 - 59	
6.30 Plurals		/10	60 - 61	
6.31 Suffix: ly		/10	62 - 63	
6.32 Suffix: ity		/10	64 - 65	
6.33 ary, ery, ory		/10	66 - 67	
6.34 ably, ibly		/10	68 - 69	
6.35 in, im, ir, il		/10	70 - 71	
6.36 ancy, ency		/10	72 - 73	

ea and ee

List **1 Write the word.**

league ______
fleece ______
appeal ______
freezer ______
seventeenth ______
coffee ______
disease ______
between ______
beneath ______
increase ______
deceased ______
proceed ______
absentee ______
tweezers ______
nominee ______
meagre ______
creature ______
easel ______
kneeling ______
employee ______

2 Name.

______ ______

3 Word clues. Which list word matches?

sheep's wool ______
to make larger ______
a person who is absent ______
competing sports teams ______
stores frozen food ______
in a lower place ______
a paid worker ______
harm to someone's health ______
small amount of something ______

4 Complete the sentence with a list word.

The sight of a plate of vegetables does not ______ to me.
I quickly packed the ice-cream into the ______ before it melted.
After having friends over, we only had a ______ amount of food left.
Dad is always grumpy before his morning ______ .
Mum said she would ______ my allowance if I completed more chores.
Jodie is my ______ for school captain.
After Saturday's game our team is at the bottom of the ______ .
Doctors treated the ______ with a course of antibiotics.

ea and ee

5 Underline the spelling mistake. Write the word correctly.

Noah sat betwean Jacob and Cheyenne in the back seat. ________

I set up my eisel and canvas at the window, ready to paint. ________

An owl is a creecher of the night. ________

She used a pair of twezers to pick the splinter from my finger. ________

His new fleese jacket kept him very warm. ________

It is my older sister's sevententh birthday tomorrow. ________

Challenge words

6 Write the word.

beacon ________

bequeath ________

feeble ________

wheedle ________

refugee ________

pedigree ________

appease ________

colleague ________

demeanour ________

chimpanzee ________

7 Meaning. Which challenge word matches?

To give someone what they want. ________

To pass on or transfer one's possessions to another. ________

To persuade someone to give you something. ________

A person who is forced to seek safety in another country. ________

To be lacking in strength. ________

A signal light that warns ships or aircraft. ________

8 Complete the sentence.

The breeder assured us the puppy was of a good p________.

She felt very f________ after being sick for so long.

The family had to stay in a r________ camp after fleeing their country.

My grandparents will b________ their house to my parents.

My brother is trying to w________ his way out of doing the dishes.

She gave the child a chocolate to a________ her.

Dad brought his work c________ home for dinner.

They have a baby c________ at the zoo.

Homophones

List **1 Write the word.**

bald ____
bawled ____
brows ____
browse ____
manner ____
manor ____
least ____
leased ____
sword ____
soared ____
hanger ____
hangar ____
rained ____
reigned ____
sealing ____
ceiling ____
marshal ____
martial ____
coward ____
cowered ____

2 Name.

[ ] [ ]

3 Chunks. Rearrange the chunks to make a list word.

er a h ng ____
se ow br ____
d al b ____
ei l c ing ____
ow s r b ____
ed ow er c ____
al sh ar m ____
er nn ma ____
wa rd co ____
ea l sed ____
ed rei gn ____

4 Word clues. Which list word matches?

cried ____
ruled ____
rented ____
drizzled ____
house ____
flew ____
cringed ____

hairless ____
eyebrows ____
blade ____
closing ____
roof ____
hook ____
skim ____

Homophones

5 Complete the sentence with the correct list words.

The pilot arrived at the ____________, and hung his jacket on a ____________. (hangar, hanger)

It never ____________ while the queen ____________. (reigned, rained)

The army ____________ knew a unique form of ____________ arts. (martial, marshal)

The ____________ ran and ____________ under his bed. (cowered, coward)

The vultures ____________ above the knight as he drew his ____________. (sword, soared)

At ____________ they have finally ____________ a house. (leased, least)

Challenge words

6 Write the word.

mussels ____________

muscles ____________

fazed ____________

phased ____________

border ____________

boarder ____________

assistants ____________

assistance ____________

bazaar ____________

bizarre ____________

7 Word clues. Which challenge word matches?

people who help ____________

an outdoor market ____________

odd or unusual ____________

seafood ____________

line around the edge ____________

part of the body ____________

gradually introduced ____________

giving support ____________

shock in a negative way ____________

8 Complete the sentence.

We went to the b____________ to buy some spices.

Playing sports has strengthened her m____________.

He was not f____________ by his brother's bad behaviour.

I completed all my tasks with the a____________ of my friend.

I drew a floral b____________ around my page.

er, est

List 1 Write the word.

List	
stranger	
brighter	
gentlest	
briefest	
swifter	
harsher	
friendliest	
toughest	
greediest	
littlest	
heavier	
jolliest	
tastiest	
funnier	
smelliest	
wittier	
skinnier	
nastiest	
prettier	
craziest	

2 Sort the words.

er	est

3 Fill in the missing letters.

brig ________ har________

gen________ gre________

swi________ tou________

fu________ joll________

he________ sme________

nas________ brie________

4 Complete the table.

little	littler	littlest
		funniest
smelly		
pretty		
friendly		
	gentler	
	nastier	
crazy		

er, est

5 Underline the spelling mistakes. Write the word correctly.

My torch is a lot breighter than your torch. ________________

We had the breefest meeting between classes. ________________

I picked the litteliest puppy from the litter. ________________

My brother is a lot funneir than my dad. ________________

Metal is usually heaveir than wood. ________________

The sun is harssher in summer than in winter. ________________

Challenge words

6 Write the word.

scarier ________________

filthiest ________________

busiest ________________

faintest ________________

healthier ________________

scarcer ________________

thirstier ________________

hungrier ________________

fiercest ________________

juiciest ________________

7 Hidden words. Find the challenge word.

sdfhdubusiestfgrdf ________________

dgvvffiercestxcvff ________________

fgfbvhungrierxfgvfg ________________

xdvgxcfvfaintestvx ________________

fgvxcvscarcerxcbvv ________________

ciestjuiciestjjuid ________________

thirehealthierhelt ________________

tierthirstierthis ________________

rreriscarierscera ________________

8 Complete the sentence.

That horror film was ________________ than the first one we watched.

I am eating lots of vegetables so I can be ________________.

I gave him the rest of my water because he was ________________ than me.

The bathroom was the ________________ room so we started cleaning there first.

I picked the ________________ peach from the tree.

Food was ________________ during the war.

Tom was ________________ than Mick, so he got the extra cheeseburger.

The beach is ________________ during the summertime.

Endings: ant, ent

List **1 Write the word.**

relevant ______
observant ______
insolent ______
strident ______
truant ______
resistant ______
reluctant ______
stagnant ______
pungent ______
ligament ______
valiant ______
indignant ______
component ______
diligent ______
consultant ______
prominent ______
despondent ______
pheasant ______
consonant ______
opulent ______

2 In a group. Write the list word that belongs in each group.

watchful, alert, ______
smelly, strong, ______
brave, heroic, ______
rude, cheeky, ______
motionless, stationary, ______
rich, luxurious, ______
dutiful, persistent, ______
guide, advisor, ______

3 Chunks. Rearrange the chunks to make a list word.

sis ta nt re ______
a me nt lig ______
i nen t m pro ______
so na nt con ______
ea sa nt ph ______
luc ta nt re ______
le va nt re ______
po ne com nt ______
de pon nt des ______

4 Meaning. Which list word means?

Harsh sounding or loud and unpleasant. ______
Feeling angry towards something that you think is unfair. ______
To show care and hard work in your duties. ______
Tissue that holds bone and cartilage together. ______
Someone whose job is to give advice to another. ______
Unhappy, depressed or low in spirits. ______
A large bird with bright feathers and a long tail. ______
Having a sharp or strong taste or smell. ______

Endings: ant, ent

5 Underline the spelling mistake. Write the word correctly.

He got into trouble for being truent from school. ______

JK Rowling is a prominant author of our time. ______

She was reluctent to go down to the basement alone. ______

The word 'on' is made up of one vowel and one consonent. ______

The mouldy cheese had a very pungant smell. ______

Vegetables are one componant of a healthy diet. ______

She felt indignent at his ridiculous accusation. ______

Her comment about maths was not relevent to our discussion on geography. ______

Challenge words

6 Write the word.

deodorant ______

adjacent ______

exuberant ______

exorbitant ______

triumphant ______

sufficient ______

translucent ______

correspondent ______

succulent ______

coherent ______

7 Word clues. Which challenge word matches?

much too high ______

next to ______

juicy, tender or tasty ______

clearly expressed ______

successful ______

enough ______

covers unpleasant smells ______

only allowing some light through ______

8 Another way to say it. Which challenge word could replace the underlined word?.

Jess didn't want to pay an <u>unreasonable</u> price for a computer. ______

The new post office is being built <u>next</u> to the old florist. ______

I picked a <u>juicy</u> orange from our neighbour's orange tree. ______

The <u>victorious</u> team stepped up to accept their medals. ______

I always put on <u>antiperspirant</u> after playing sport. ______

I couldn't understand her as she wasn't being very <u>clear</u>. ______

Plurals

List **1 Write the word.**

services ____________
examples ____________
sandwiches ____________
stopwatches ____________
chocolates ____________
elephants ____________
feathers ____________
thousands ____________
eyelashes ____________
museums ____________
squirrels ____________
guesses ____________
liquids ____________
stomachs ____________
cockroaches ____________
bonuses ____________
tortoises ____________
avocados ____________
governors ____________
saucers ____________

2 Complete the table.

service	services
bonus	
eyelash	
stopwatch	
	elephants
sandwich	
example	
avocado	

3 Chunks. Rearrange the chunks to make a list word.

wi es ch d san ____________
la sh es eye ____________
nu bo ses ____________
er nors gov ____________
u ir rel s sq ____________
co tes cho la ____________
se um s mu ____________
ma chs sto ____________
ck ro es ach co ____________
op tch wa st es ____________

4 Complete the sentence with a list word.

The rare parrot had brilliant blue and purple ____________.
I was extremely impressed with the many ____________ that the hotel offered.
Our apartment had so many ____________ we had to call pest control.
We needed three ____________ to make guacamole for our nachos.
We had three ____________ to figure out how many buttons were in the jar.
There are ____________ of hairs on your head.
____________ use their trunks to scoop water and food into their mouths.
Tyrannosaurus Rex and Velociraptor are two ____________ of carnivorous dinosaurs.

Plurals

5 Missing syllable. Write the missing syllable.

ele_______

ex_______ples

muse_______

avo_______dos

feath_______

_______vices

_______toises

_______nuses

_______rells

sau_______

cock_______es

choc_______lates

6 Unscramble these list words.

ndchwiessa _______________

ndsousath _______________

chmatoss _______________

orsrevogn _______________

qiiusdl _______________

eshasleey _______________

Challenge words

7 Write the word.

differences _______________

orchestras _______________

stilettos _______________

languages _______________

complexes _______________

syllabuses _______________

carcasses _______________

addresses _______________

carriages _______________

consequences _______________

8 Hidden words. Find the challenge word.

eexoecomplexescoee _______________

ssesdaddressesadda _______________

ssscrcarcassescraesa _______________

ffesnedifferencesffes _______________

bbsuesyllabusesllasy _______________

abrocorchestrasguyg _______________

jgyuucarriagesjuoi _______________

hjygstilettosltojbgg _______________

okojlanguagesjhgkiu _______________

hbugconsequenceshu _______________

9 Complete the sentence.

They have decided to update the maths and English _______________ next year.

Over one hundred _______________ have played at the Opera House.

There are usually eight _______________ for each train.

There are many _______________ between cats and dogs.

Our teacher told us we would not like the _______________ if we didn't complete our homework.

Wearing a pair of _______________ made it hard for her to walk.

Our foreign exchange student can speak three different _______________.

Suffixes: er, or

List **1 Write the word.**

creator ______
villager ______
explorer ______
inspector ______
jeweller ______
protector ______
beginner ______
passenger ______
newcomer ______
entertainer ______
murderer ______
researcher ______
wanderer ______
supplier ______
governor ______
professor ______
examiner ______
fumigator ______
designer ______
challenger ______

2 In a group. Write the list word that belongs in each group.

nomad, traveller, ______
trader, seller, ______
university, teacher, ______
termites, exterminator, ______
performer, comedian, ______
guardian, warden, ______
pioneer, seeker, ______
novice, apprentice, ______

3 Missing letter. Write the missing letters.

vil______	ins______
______rcher	w______erer
______ssor	______gner
cha______	exa______
exp______	cre______
beg______	m______erer
______omer	gov______
______gator	pas______
enter______	pro______

4 Word clues. Which list word matches?

a person who has taken a life ______
one who makes necklaces and rings ______
one who entertains ______
one who marks exams ______
a person who travels but doesn't drive ______
someone who moves about with no purpose ______
the head of an organisation ______

Suffixes: er, or

5 Complete the sentence with a list word.

Matthew Flinders was the first ______________ to sail right round Australia.

Thomas was a ______________ to our class, so we made him feel welcome.

Farmer Ned is the ______________ of our shop's fresh fruit and vegetables.

When we found termites, we had to hire a ______________.

Mum works as a graphic ______________ for a homewares magazine.

My uncle is an English ______________ who works at the local university.

The undefeated boxing champion is waiting for his next ______________.

A fire ______________ visited the school to install new smoke alarms.

Challenge words

6 Write the word.

conqueror ______________

astronomer ______________

interpreter ______________

counsellor ______________

interviewer ______________

philosopher ______________

practitioner ______________

commissioner ______________

photographer ______________

choreographer ______________

7 Word clues. Which challenge word matches?

one who gives advice ______________

one who takes photos ______________

one who defeats another ______________

one who creates dance movements ______________

one who can translate one language into another ______________

someone who studies the universe ______________

someone practising a trade, occupation or profession ______________

8 Complete the sentence.

Confucius is an ancient Chinese ______________.

She is employed by the government to be an ______________ for international clients.

They hired a ______________ to take photos on their wedding day.

The ______________ was pleased with the progress of his dance group.

Mariah went to the school ______________ to talk about how she was feeling.

Vowels

List **1 Write the word.**

altitude ____
elevate ____
accommodate ____
ventilate ____
mosquito ____
italicise ____
exaggerate ____
semicolon ____
maritime ____
apologise ____
icicle ____
eliminate ____
magnitude ____
concede ____
retrospect ____
exonerate ____
radiate ____
sacrifice ____
emphasise ____
mundane ____

2 Name.

;

3 Chunks. Rearrange the chunks to make a list word.

te com mo ac da ____
va te e el ____
i mo to squ ____
po gise lo a ____
cri sa ce fi ____
i lon co sem ____
ni mag tude ____
ti i me mar ____
ti ven te la ____
na te lim i e ____

4 Meaning. Which list word means?

The height of a thing above the earth or sea level. ____
To make something appear larger or more important. ____
Cause fresh air to enter or circulate an interior space. ____
To say sorry for the wrong that one has done. ____
To free someone from blame. ____
Reflection on a past event. ____
Not interesting or exciting. ____
To raise or lift something to a higher position. ____

Vowels

5 Underline the spelling mistake. Write the word correctly.

The plane was flying at an altitoode of 15 000 metres. ______

In retrospekt, I should have known he would double cross me. ______

I find washing the dishes a mundaine chore. ______

It was so cold, I snapped an icycle off the bathroom tap. ______

In the end, I had to consede that she was right. ______

The court voted to exonerayte the innocent man. ______

Grandpa tends to exagerate the details of his stories. ______

We hoped that the fire would raydiate heat throughout the house. ______

Challenge words

6 Write the word.

insinuate ______

instigate ______

accumulate ______

insoluble ______

precipitate ______

illuminate ______

catastrophe ______

insulate ______

placate ______

tactile ______

7 Meaning. Which challenge word matches?

To collect or gather. ______

To purposely provoke. ______

Impossible to dissolve. ______

To calm down or pacify. ______

To subtly suggest. ______

Having to do with the sense of touch. ______

To make something happen suddenly. ______

An event that brings harm or suffering. ______

8 Another way to say it. Which challenge word could replace the underlined word?

I lit a candle to <u>light</u> the room. ______

She tried to <u>imply</u> that I was the one who stole her necklace. ______

The cyclone was a <u>disaster</u> for the whole city. ______

I always manage to <u>collect</u> more things than I need. ______

I tried to <u>start</u> a fight, but he just walked away. ______

I hoped to <u>appease</u> him by doing the dishes. ______

Suffixes: ful, less

List **1 Write the word.**

blissful ____________
stainless ____________
limitless ____________
spotless ____________
blameless ____________
listless ____________
selfless ____________
shapeless ____________
frightful ____________
speechless ____________
pitiful ____________
resentful ____________
meaningless ____________
spiteful ____________
flawless ____________
senseless ____________
boundless ____________
dreadful ____________
ruthless ____________
watchful ____________

2 Sort the words.

ful	less

3 Unscramble these list words.

ainstessl ____________
itefulps ____________
sseltimil ____________
ghtluffri ____________
amlelessb ____________
entserulf ____________

4 Missing letters. Write the missing letters.

res____________
spi____________
lim____________
sha____________
dre____________
rut____________
sta____________
sen____________

5 Chunks. Rearrange the letters to make a list word.

le se ss sen ____________
ead ful dr ____________
ful re sent ____________
le ch ss ee sp ____________
le ape sh ss ____________
ame ss bl le ____________
ss it le lim ____________

Suffixes: ful, less

6 Underline the spelling mistakes. Write the word correctly.

The news was so shocking that I was momentarily spechless. ______

Her senseles mistake could have serious consequences. ______

The diamond in her ring was completely floorless. ______

I spent all day cleaning until the house was spotles. ______

Our new fridge is made of steinless steel. ______

The road was blocked because of a dreedful accident. ______

The friteful noise kept me awake all night. ______

Challenge words

7 Write the word.

merciful ______

purposeful ______

deceitful ______

uneventful ______

disrespectful ______

teaspoonful ______

effortless ______

expressionless ______

motionless ______

resourceful ______

8 Hidden words. Find the challenge word.

ssleeexpressionlesssigd ______

fjhumotionlessshdfgb ______

sgyeffortlesssdsjhf ______

shfypurposefuldgghbj ______

sjhgdisrespectfuldfgy ______

dfbdymercifulfdbyu ______

snudteaspoonfuldnby ______

ffusresourcefulsure ______

ventfuneventfuleven ______

fuldeceitfuldecet ______

9 Complete the sentence.

He hoped the judge would be m______ with his sentence.

He was put in detention for his d______ attitude.

Mum put a t______ of honey into my tea to soothe my sore throat.

I spent an u______ weekend reading my new book.

The high jumper cleared the bar with e______ ease.

I couldn't tell what she was thinking as her face was e______.

un, mis, dis

List

unlikely
unlimited
misread
disregard
misfired
disbelief
disallowed
unwelcome
unleash
disorderly
misshapen
disapproval
unsuitable
unrealistic
displeasure
disagreement
unattractive
misfielded
unavoidable
unreasonable

1 Write the word.

______
______
______
______
______
______
______
______
______
______
______
______
______
______
______
______
______
______
______
______

2 Chunks. Rearrange the chunks to make a list word.

or der dis ly ______
sui ta un ble ______
a gree dis nt me ______
voi a un ble da ______
rea son ble un a ______
wel co un me ______
pp val ro dis a ______
a ttr ac ve ti un ______

3 Fill in the missing letters.

______likely ______read
______approval ______leash
______agreement ______pleasure
______suitable ______avoidable
______fielded ______regard
______reasonable ______realistic
______limited ______shapen
______welcome ______attractive

4 Sort the words.

un	dis	mis

5 Underline the spelling mistakes. Write the word correctly.

I disread the directions and headed east instead of west. ______________

At the hotel we had mislimited access to the pool, gym and spa. ______________

A jacket is dissuitable in hot weather. ______________

Seeing gum on the bottom of my shoe was an miswelcome sight. ______________

We are not allowed to disleash our dogs in the national park. ______________

Books were stacked in misorderly piles all over her desk. ______________

I tried to work my disshapen ball of clay back into shape. ______________

My sister annoyed me all day, much to my unpleasure. ______________

I found her arrogant behaviour extremely disattractive. ______________

Challenge words

6 Write the word.

unsuccessful ______________

disqualification ______________

misdiagnose ______________

unmistakable ______________

unreliable ______________

unofficial ______________

unprecedented ______________

misrepresented ______________

misidentified ______________

miscalculation ______________

7 Hidden words. Find the challenge word.

fgbmiscalculationfgn ______________

idnmisidentifieddfgn ______________

jhgfgunofficialfgfjh ______________

nfduunreliabledfg ______________

niudisqualificationkd ______________

seemisrepresentedmir ______________

aleunmistakablemsi ______________

sukunsuccessfulccsue ______________

neidmisdiagnosemsei ______________

isbpunprecedentedgrs ______________

8 Complete the sentence.

The doctor was careful as he did not want to ______________ his patient's illness.

Cheating in an exam could lead to a ______________.

In the crowd, her bright blue hair was ______________.

At first they were ______________, but eventually they started to see results.

I wouldn't count on him, as he is very ______________.

His speech completely ______________ the views expressed in his book.

ai and ay

List **1 Write the word.**

afraid ______
raised ______
crayon ______
mermaid ______
tailor ______
decay ______
praise ______
maintain ______
mayonnaise ______
sustain ______
attain ______
domain ______
remained ______
failure ______
mayhem ______
foray ______
betrayal ______
wraith ______
portrayal ______
curtail ______

2 Name.

CRAYON
YELLOW

[ ] [ ]

3 Unscramble these list words.

desair ______
ailort ______
aiprse ______
aiainmnt ______
ainmod ______
aierulf ______
aymehm ______
ayrof ______
aylartrop ______
ayesiannom ______

4 Word clues. Which list word matches?

something you put on a sandwich ______
someone who makes or alters clothing ______
a mythical sea creature ______
utter chaos ______
someone's land ______
to rot ______
a ghost or spirit ______
to make shorter or cut off ______

ai and ay

5 Underline the spelling mistakes. Write the word correctly.

I couldn't go all the way to the top as I am afrayd of heights. ____________

I wrote my name on a piece of paper in bright pink craion. ____________

A mermayd is a mythical creature that lives in the ocean. ____________

Mum was so impressed that she decided to rayse my allowance. ____________

There was utter maihem when a spider fell on Maddy's head. ____________

The taylor made my brother a suit for the wedding. ____________

It is important that students help to mayntayn the school's gardens. ____________

Challenge words

6 Write the word.

bailiff ____________

appraisal ____________

bayonet ____________

stowaway ____________

disarray ____________

liaise ____________

assailant ____________

ascertain ____________

plaintiff ____________

ailment ____________

7 Word clues. Which challenge word matches?

a sickness or disorder ____________

a weapon ____________

an attacker ____________

an officer of the law ____________

a state of confusion ____________

to make sure of ____________

a person who hides on a ship, train or aeroplane ____________

one who initiates a lawsuit ____________

a judgement of something's value ____________

8 Complete the sentence.

The doctor is running tests to ____________ the cause of her illness.

His ____________ prevented him from competing in the cross country race.

The ____________ was caught by police and put on trial for his crimes.

My hair was in complete ____________ after I crawled through the bush.

The ____________ is claiming the defendant purposely tried to wreck her bicycle.

The ____________ hid inside a giant barrel, hoping no one would find him.

Word building

List **1 Write the word.**

compare ________
comparing ________
compared ________
comparison ________
comparative ________
correct ________
correcting ________
corrected ________
correction ________
incorrectly ________
shrink ________
shrinking ________
shrank ________
shrunken ________
shrinkage ________
value ________
valued ________
valuing ________
valuable ________
valuation ________

2 Unscramble these list words.

nnkeurhs ________
cedtrroec ________
aknhrs ________
knirhs ________
yltcerrocni ________
alveud ________
raavitemocp ________
paerdomc ________

3 Chunks. Rearrange the chunks to make a list word.

in ge ka shr ________
a tive com par ________
re co pa m ________
ted rec cor ________
ink ing shr ________
un shr ken ________
u ble a val ________
cor ly in rect ________
tion u val a ________

4 Meaning. Which list word means?

To make smaller in size or amount. ________
To fix mistakes, to make something right. ________
The worth, usefulness or importance of something. ________
Making right. ________
To estimate, measure or describe the similarities or differences between two or more things. ________

Word building

5 Complete each sentence with a list word.

My brand new t-shirt ______________ two sizes in the wash.

I gave my ______________ shirt to my little brother, because it no longer fitted me.

I hope my new clothes don't ______________ in the wash.

The auctioneer ______________ the vintage dressing table at $500.

They hoped the ______________ of the house would be over a million dollars.

I got nervous when they were ______________ the house.

When I ______________ the computers, I found there wasn't much difference between them.

Challenge words

6 Write the word.

navigate ______________

navigating ______________

navigator ______________

navigation ______________

circumnavigation ______________

continue ______________

discontinued ______________

continually ______________

continuity ______________

continuation ______________

7 Hidden words. Find the challenge word.

allyucontinuallycon ______________

aigntnavigatingvahd ______________

uityrcontinuitycont ______________

autincontinuationcon ______________

fkgnonavigatoragte ______________

tueddiscontinuedcons ______________

atigonavigationnaiv ______________

usuecontinueskdn ______________

sdgbjgnavigatedghr ______________

gatcircumnavigation ______________

8 Complete the sentence.

The sailors had to ______________ their way through treacherous waters.

The plane's ______________ consulted the compass to make sure they were on course.

Matthew Flinders was the first man to complete a ______________ of Australia.

After losing their compass, they had to rely on ______________ by the stars.

I was heartbroken when they ______________ my favourite cartoon.

Dad wasn't very good at ______________ us home.

Suffix: ic

List **1 Write the word.**

traffic ______
domestic ______
gigantic ______
majestic ______
energetic ______
cosmetic ______
symbolic ______
organic ______
climatic ______
economic ______
synthetic ______
electronic ______
scenic ______
idealistic ______
sarcastic ______
chaotic ______
geometric ______
dynamic ______
patriotic ______
allergic ______

2 In a group. Write the list word that belongs in each group.

man-made, artificial, ______
squares, triangles, ______
cars, roads, ______
huge, big, ______
technology, electricity, ______
loyalty, allegiance, ______
beauty, make-up, ______

3 Chunks. Rearrange the chunks to make a list word.

o cha tic ______
mes tic do ______
gan gi tic ______
the tic n sy ______
o me ge tric ______
nom o ic ec ______
ma cli tic ______
ge er en tic ______

4 Word clues. Which list word matches?

having impressive beauty or scale ______
relating to home or family ______
man-made from chemicals; artificial ______
produced without the use of pesticides ______
natural or beautiful scenery ______
normal weather conditions ______
completely disordered or disorganised ______
of a very great size or extent ______

Suffix: ic

5 Complete each sentence with a list word.

We arrived at the party late because we were stuck in ________________.

Mum's favourite ________________ brand just released a new lipstick colour.

A rose is often ________________ of love.

My mobile phone is an ________________ device.

I stayed away from her peanut butter sandwich as I am ________________ to nuts.

We decided to take the ________________ route along the beautiful Australian coast.

His ________________ comment hurt my feelings.

I could tell by his ________________ response that he felt passionately about the campaign.

Polyester and nylon are both ________________ fabrics.

Challenge words

6 Write the word.

epidemic ________________

characteristic ________________

systematic ________________

emphatic ________________

apologetic ________________

rhythmic ________________

aristocratic ________________

therapeutic ________________

eccentric ________________

philharmonic ________________

7 Word clues. Which challenge word matches?

capable of healing ________________

expressing regret ________________

odd or peculiar ________________

not random or chaotic ________________

a distinguishing feature ________________

rapidly spreading disease ________________

relating to an orchestra ________________

having a regular pattern of sounds ________________

8 Complete the sentence.

The doctors were working hard to find a way to control the ________________.

After a stressful week I had a ________________ massage.

It was the ________________ beat of the music that led me to the dance floor.

Her confident attitude is her best ________________.

Compound words

List | **1 Write the word.**

southwest ______
household ______
northeast ______
thunderstorm ______
whitewash ______
grandchildren ______
soundproof ______
scarecrow ______
firebreak ______
marketplace ______
great-grandfather ______
mother-in-law ______
eyewitness ______
wheelchair ______
sightseeing ______
headdress ______
sandcastle ______
gentlemen ______
thanksgiving ______
guideline ______

2 Missing letters. Write the missing letters.

nort______
______orm
______stle
sout______
hea______
______oof
scar______
______ace

3 In a group. Write the list word that belongs in each group.

paint, white, ______
bazaar, stalls, ______
bandana, headband, ______
birds, crops, ______
beach, buckets, ______
silent, mute, ______
procedure, instruction, ______
observer, bystander, ______

4 Word clues. Which list word matches?

heavy wind, rain and lightning ______
constructed at the beach ______
helps people who are unable to walk ______
someone who is often part of criminal trials ______
prevents sound ______
the people who live in a house ______
descendants ______
something tourists do ______

Compound words

5 Underline the spelling mistakes. Write the word correctly.

When we go on holiday, we do a lot of siteseeing. ________

When I marry Tim, Angela will become my mother-in-lore. ________

Thanksgiveing is held on the fourth Thursday of November. ________

The polite gentelman offered me his coat when I was cold. ________

We bought spices and dried fruit from the marcketplace. ________

If you do not stick to the assessment gidelines, you will lose marks. ________

Challenge words

6 Write the word.

upheaval ________

afterimage ________

masterpiece ________

coldblooded ________

superimpose ________

trustworthy ________

overboard ________

viewpoint ________

beachcomber ________

weatherproof ________

7 Word clues. Which challenge word matches?

a fine work of art ________

dependable or reliable ________

fall from a boat ________

to set on top of an image ________

able to resist weather damage ________

a collector of goods washed ashore ________

blood that changes with the temperature of the air or water ________

8 Complete the sentence.

The novel was written from the ________ of the protagonist.

Snakes, lizards and fish are all ________ creatures.

The pirates cut loose their prisoners before throwing them ________.

He only taught his most ________ friends his secret language.

I tried to ________ a picture of my face over that of my friend's face.

I kept seeing the ________ of the painting long after I looked away.

Loan words

List **1 Write the word.**

tempo ____
torso ____
stanza ____
tirade ____
cello ____
parole ____
elite ____
dessert ____
garage ____
arsenal ____
debut ____
broccoli ____
fiancée ____
petite ____
prestige ____
gondola ____
morale ____
battalion ____
concerto ____
confetti ____

2 Name.

3 In a group. Write the list word that belongs in each group.

pumpkin, cauliflower, ____
verse, chorus, ____
small, tiny, ____
violin, viola, ____
canoe, kayak, ____
rhythm, speed, ____

4 Meaning. Which list word means?

A group of lines that make up one section of a poem. ____
A large group of soldiers. ____
The human body from the neck to the hips. ____
The speed at which music is played. ____
A large musical instrument with four strings. ____
Sweet food served at the end of a meal. ____
A narrow boat, propelled using a long pole. ____
Small pieces of coloured paper thrown in the air during parties or parades. ____

5 Complete the sentence with a list word.

The dancers twirled as the ________________ of the music increased.

I was asked to read the first ________________ of my poem to the class.

Mum wants me to learn the ________________, but I would rather play the saxophone.

For ________________ we had apple pie with homemade vanilla ice-cream.

The upcoming artist was about to release her ________________ album.

She needs the smallest size as she has a ________________ frame.

The ________________ took us along the canals of Venice.

Challenge words

6 Write the word.

façade	________________
souvenir	________________
zucchini	________________
chagrin	________________
gourmet	________________
cuisine	________________
croissant	________________
pirouette	________________
crescendo	________________
picturesque	________________

7 Hidden words. Find the challenge word.

fgdkhfgchagrindjgnfg	________________
eutheujpirouettedjgbu	________________
sdhduscrescendosdu	________________
ngdufgsouvenirfdfj	________________
dfhgugourmetfnbjf	________________
gnfigicuisinedjgn	________________
saquuepicturesquepictt	________________
sssoicroissantcrosn	________________
hinihzucchiniccchii	________________
cadefaçadefaec	________________

8 Complete the sentence.

We sat outside to watch the ________________ sunset.

I had a hot chocolate and a ________________ for breakfast.

The audience was awed by the dancer's ________________.

I bought a ________________ from each country I visited.

We had a celebratory dinner at a lovely ________________ restaurant.

The orchestra starts softly then builds into a ________________.

ie and ei

List	1 Write the word.
cashier	
fiend	
feint	
abseil	
neither	
heiress	
believing	
fiery	
deceive	
eerie	
skein	
client	
receiving	
heirloom	
heifer	
forfeit	
weir	
anxiety	
receipt	
beige	

2 Missing letters. Write the missing letters.

_ eir _ o _ _	re _ _ _ _ t
_ n _ ie _ y	he _ _ _ _
_ _ _ fei _	cl _ _ _ t
_ eir _ _ s	fi _ _ y
_ _ ceiv _	c _ _ h _ _ r
_ _ lie _ _ _ g	b _ _ g _
_ _ _ eil	we _ _
_ ein _	_ _ cei _ _ _ _
_ _ rie	sk _ _ _
_ ei _ _ er	fi _ _ d

3 Unscramble these words.

ndeif ______

ryefi ______

lintec ______

reefih ______

shaceir ______

geeib ______

peeictr ______

nieks ______

4 Word clues. Which list word matches?

a female who will inherit another's possessions ______

mysterious, frightening or weird ______

a false move meant to trick an opponent ______

paper showing money given or received ______

descending a rock surface using ropes ______

cruelly malicious person ______

an object passed down through generations ______

to lose by doing something wrong ______

5 Complete each sentence with a list word.

We paid the ________________ for our groceries.

The ________________ was set to inherit her uncle's large estate and wealth.

On the school camp I was too afraid to ________________ down the steep cliff.

I could not return the shoes because I lost my ________________.

The firefighter rescued the family from the ________________ building.

We didn't have enough players, so we had to ________________ the game.

I was full of ________________ before our English exam.

Challenge words

6 Write the word.

frontier ________________

seismic ________________

heinous ________________

eiderdown ________________

surfeit ________________

caffeine ________________

seizure ________________

aggrieved ________________

counterfeit ________________

cuneiform ________________

7 Word clues. Which challenge word matches?

used to fill a quilt ________________

relating to earthquakes ________________

something fake made to look real ________________

a border between two countries ________________

an excessive amount of something ________________

a substance that causes a person to stay awake ________________

8 Another way to say it. Which challenge word could replace the underlined word.

After the holidays we had a <u>surplus</u> of food. ________________

She was feeling <u>hurt</u> after her brother made fun of her. ________________

The soldiers fought on the <u>border</u> between the warring countries. ________________

He was prosecuted for the <u>monstrous</u> crimes he had committed. ________________

The <u>capture</u> of native land started protests in the local community. ________________

The police were trying to control the outbreak of <u>fake</u> banknotes. ________________

able, ible

List — **1 Write the word.**

available ______
notable ______
memorable ______
remarkable ______
fashionable ______
perishable ______
responsible ______
adaptable ______
profitable ______
audible ______
charitable ______
miserable ______
disposable ______
forcible ______
admissible ______
plausible ______
applicable ______
convertible ______
commendable ______
understandable ______

2 In a group. Write the list word that belongs in each group.

unhappy, depressed, ______
stylish, trendy, ______
believable, probable, ______
clear, logical, ______
extraordinary, amazing, ______
aggressive, violent, ______
impressive, important, ______

3 Chunks. Rearrange the chunks to make a list word.

spon ble si re ______
men da ble com ______
ar it ble a ch ______
fi ble ta pro ______
ver ble ti con ______
der da stan ble un ______
ka mar ble re ______
dap ble ta a ______

4 Word clues. Which list word matches?

able to adjust to changing conditions ______
able to be heard ______
a car with a roof that can fold down ______
current, popular style ______
likely to rot in a short time ______
generous in actions or donations ______
to be very unhappy ______
easily remembered ______

able, ible

5 Underline the spelling mistakes. Write the word correctly.

There were no more rooms availible at the hotel. ______

The dog ate my homework is not a plausable excuse. ______

The colour lilac is very fashionible this month. ______

She talked so quietly she was barely audable. ______

It is simply remarkible the way she can paint with her toes! ______

Meeting my favourite author was a memorible experience. ______

Mother told me I had to be responsable for my actions. ______

Lucy helped her mother weed the garden as she was feeling charitible.

______

Challenge words

6 Write the word.

foreseeable ______
comparable ______
permissible ______
contemptible ______
justifiable ______
digestible ______
reproducible ______
perceptible ______
intelligible ______
comprehensible ______

7 Hidden words. Find the challenge word.

gudfjustifiabledsfhbk ______
ndgcomprehensiblesd ______
shbfdigestibledfsed ______
gdyupermissiblesdkj ______
dksnforeseeablesdfj ______
jbfucontemptiblefdg ______
ibbleintelligibleinttll ______
tiblperceptiblepecep ______
vibreproduciblererop ______
belcomparablecoome ______

8 Word clues. Which challenge word matches?

can be seen in advance ______
can be understood ______
will be allowed ______
capable of being absorbed by the body ______
able to be copied ______

igh, eigh, aigh

List **1 Write the word.**

alight ______
blight ______
slightly ______
almighty ______
brighten ______
midnight ______
headlight ______
eighty-eight ______
fortnightly ______
firefighter ______
sprightly ______
airfreight ______
knighted ______
candlelight ______
floodlights ______
mightiest ______
forthright ______
frightening ______
rightfully ______
copyright ______

2 Name.

3 Missing letters. Write the missing letters.

al _ _ _ t	fl _ _ _ li _ _ _ _
spr _ _ _ _ ly	ri _ _ _ fu _ _ _
m _ _ _ _ _ _ _ st	co _ _ ri _ _ _
bl _ _ _ t	sl _ _ _ t _ _
air _ _ _ _ _ _ _ t	br _ _ _ t _ _
fi _ _ fi _ _ _ _ _ _	kn _ _ _ t _ _

4 Word clues. Which list word matches?

twelve o'clock at night ______
lights that shine wide beams of light ______
a bright light on the front of a vehicle ______
goods shipped by plane ______
every two weeks ______
legal right to publish or distribute one's written work ______
lively or energetic ______
one who fights fires ______

igh, eigh, aigh

5 Underline the spelling mistake. Write the word correctly.

It was almost midneight by the time I finally got to sleep. ________

Tomorrow my grandmother will be aighty-aight years old. ________

Having a large spider in your room is a freightening experience. ________

Since I paid for it, it is reightfully mine. ________

The firefeighter ran towards the flames, hose in hand. ________

Her work was protected by copyreight. ________

The newsletter comes out fortneightly. ________

Her forthreight manner makes people uncomfortable. ________

Challenge words

6 Write the word.

enlighten ________

insightful ________

delightfully ________

nightmarish ________

straightener ________

weightlifting ________

farsighted ________

featherweight ________

straightforward ________

neighbourliness ________

7 Word clues. Which challenge word matches?

frank or honest ________

not heavy ________

to give knowledge ________

not able to see objects up close ________

a device used for styling hair ________

having a deep understanding ________

8 Complete the sentence.

She was praised for her ________ remark about the main character.

Our community prides itself on its ________.

He is a lot stronger since he started ________.

I won the championship in the ________ boxing division.

She uses a ________ to smooth her curly hair.

Linda wears glasses as she is ________.

Suffix: ous

List **1 Write the word.**

luxurious ____________
ravenous ____________
notorious ____________
tenacious ____________
venomous ____________
vivacious ____________
obnoxious ____________
momentous ____________
tremendous ____________
amphibious ____________
zealous ____________
precarious ____________
voracious ____________
ambiguous ____________
impervious ____________
tumultuous ____________
anonymous ____________
conspicuous ____________
contentious ____________
contemptuous ____________

2 In a group. Write the list word that belongs in each group.

rich, lavish, ____________
poisonous, toxic, ____________
vague, unclear, ____________
famous, renowned, ____________
starving, hungry, ____________
disagreeable, nasty, ____________
unknown, mysterious, ____________

3 Chunks. Rearrange the chunks to make a list word.

nous ra ve ____________
cari pre ous ____________
temp ous tu con ____________
ous tre mend ____________
tor ous no i ____________
bi ous am phi ____________
ci ten ous a ____________
cu con spi ous ____________
mul tu tu ous ____________

4 Meaning. Which list word means?

Able to live on land and in water. ____________
Very hungry or starving. ____________
Having an unknown name or identity. ____________
Full of noise, commotion or chaos. ____________
Not affected by anything. ____________
Something that is not secure, or considered dangerous. ____________
Having more than one meaning. ____________
Something that is obvious or easily seen. ____________

Suffix: ous

5 Complete each sentence with a list word.

The box jellyfish is the world's most v__________________ creature.

It was an a__________________ witness that reported the crime.

He was standing on top of the ladder in a p__________________ position.

I was so r__________________, I ate four sandwiches and the leftover spaghetti.

His a__________________ answer left us all very confused.

A frog is an a__________________ creature.

Everyone put in a t__________________ effort.

We stayed in a l__________________ new hotel suite.

I am i__________________ to his nasty comments.

Challenge words

6 Write the word.

voluminous __________________

precipitous __________________

prestigious __________________

ostentatious __________________

simultaneous __________________

unscrupulous __________________

synonymous __________________

instantaneous __________________

unpretentious __________________

presumptuous __________________

7 Word clues. Which challenge word matches?

done at the same time __________________

highly esteemed __________________

great size or quantity __________________

no moral principals __________________

very steep __________________

a showy display designed to impress __________________

happening immediately __________________

8 Complete the sentence.

The word 'attempt' is s__________________ with 'try'.

She is very u__________________; she never tries to show off.

It was a p__________________ climb up the mountain, but we made it!

Her parents were very proud when she won the p__________________ award.

It was p__________________ of her to ask such a personal question.

oa and ow

List **1 Write the word.**

List	
foamy	
shown	
growth	
throat	
burrows	
thrown	
hollow	
coast	
cockroach	
marshmallow	
cocoa	
broach	
loathe	
coaxes	
marrow	
approach	
poacher	
widower	
cloakroom	
bellowing	

2 Sort the words.

oa	ow

3 Name.

4 Meaning. Which list word means?

A powder made by grinding the dried seeds of the cacao tree. ______

To come near to someone or something. ______

One who hunts illegally on another's property. ______

A man whose wife has passed away and has not remarried. ______

Tunnels dug by animals as a shelter or hiding place. ______

The land next to the sea. ______

To hate or dislike very much. ______

To have an empty place inside. ______

oa and ow

5 Complete each sentence with a list word.

Lack of water will affect the plant's ________________.

We travelled to the north ________________ of the island and stayed at a resort.

My grandmother put a ________________ into my hot cocoa as a treat.

My ________________ was sore and scratchy from talking all day long.

When they cut the tree, they discovered it was ________________ inside.

Foxes and rabbits live in ________________ under the ground.

After the storm, the sea was rough and ________________.

The ________________ has trapped the animals illegally.

Challenge words

6 Write the word.

boastful ________________

charcoal ________________

wallows ________________

foreshadow ________________

petticoat ________________

encroach ________________

reproach ________________

loathsome ________________

unknowingly ________________

irreproachable ________________

7 Hidden words. Find the challenge word.

dfgfencroachddfhb ________________

hgirreproachablede ________________

djgicharcoalcvj ________________

dskjghboastfulfgf ________________

shauforeshadowfgn ________________

djguloathsomedfds ________________

inyunknowinglyknu ________________

caotpetticoatttipe ________________

lloswwallowsaalow ________________

8 Another way to say it. Which list word could replace the underlined word?

I did not want to <u>intrude</u> on his privacy. ________________

The event seemed to <u>forecast</u> more trouble to come. ________________

On the farm the pig always <u>rolls</u> in the mud. ________________

There was a <u>disgusting</u> smell coming from the fridge. ________________

Mum will <u>chide</u> me for not taking out the rubbish. ________________

I <u>ignorantly</u> left the ice-cream out and it all melted. ________________

Greek origins

List — 1 Write the word.

cycling
bicycle
cyclone
motorcycle
comedy
melody
parody
iconic
physics
hydrate
academy
physical
botanical
dehydrate
hydrogen
exhilarate
hilarity
hydrant
oxygen
encyclopedia

2 Name.

3 Unscramble the list words.

ydorap
ayadmec
txahearlie
gnhdoyer
tacalnibo
mcyedo
etardyhed
dthryan
artiyilh
niicco
aretyhd
oortmccyel

4 Word clues. Which list word matches?

relating to plants
a two wheel vehicle
the study of matter and energy
musical sounds
an amusing imitation
to remove water
an informative book
a pipe from which water can be drawn

5 Underline the spelling mistakes. Write the word correctly.

Sydney's Opera House is an ikonic landmark. ______

There was great hilerity when Alex slipped on a banana skin. ______

The song's meledy sounded very familiar. ______

We ate lunch under a tree in the Botanicel Gardens. ______

We breathe in oxigen and breathe out carbon dioxide. ______

We drank lots of water to hydraet ourselves on the hot day. ______

His amazing portfolio won him a place at a prestigious art acadimy. ______

Challenge words

6 Write the word.

physiology ______

cyclonic ______

rhapsody ______

dysentery ______

dysfunctional ______

physically ______

dehydration ______

hydroelectric ______

hydraulic ______

carbohydrate ______

7 Hidden words. Find the challenge word.

hisophysiologyhdsgou ______

sjgbudhydroelectricodfgi ______

defuscarbohydratessgsd ______

dgnbuphysicallydgd ______

dyssdysfunctionalfudction ______

8 Word clues. Which challenge word matches?

an infectious disease ______

to lose water

moved or operated by water ______

the science of living things ______

an irregular musical composition ______

a compound made of carbon, hydrogen and oxygen ______

describes a storm with strong winds ______

re, de, pre

List

1 Write the word.

- prefix ____________
- reopen ____________
- predates ____________
- preview ____________
- reappear ____________
- deactivate ____________
- preschool ____________
- relocate ____________
- reconstruct ____________
- rediscover ____________
- demobilise ____________
- reschedule ____________
- reinstate ____________
- reinforce ____________
- revalued ____________
- redesign ____________
- reassure ____________
- deregulate ____________
- reorganise ____________
- reprocess ____________

2 Unscramble the list words.

- onrecuctstr ____________
- ssecorper ____________
- etalgurede ____________
- etavitecad ____________
- atsedrep ____________
- wievper ____________
- oolscherp ____________
- mobediilse ____________
- luaedver ____________

3 Chunks. Rearrange the chunks to make a list word.

- or ga se ni re ____________
- pro ss ce re ____________
- reg te la u de ____________
- for in ce re ____________
- bi li mo se de ____________
- ver dis re co ____________
- act va te i de ____________
- str con uct re ____________

4 Complete each sentence with a list word.

We had to ____________ the fire alarm as it went off for no reason.

We had to ____________ our soccer match because of the rain.

They had to ____________ the building to withstand earthquakes.

The time of the dinosaurs ____________ the Ice Age.

He made the rabbit disappear and then ____________ on my shoulder!

I tried to ____________ her that everything would be alright.

A ____________ changes the meaning of a word.

Next year we are going to ____________ to the United States.

re, de, pre

5 Underline the spelling mistakes. Write the word correctly.

The school employed a local artist to ridesign the school banner. ____________

On the weekend I plan to reorganyse my bedroom. ____________

Our local government decided to reinstaite our old mayor. ____________

They have decided to reopan the old roller coaster park. ____________

We had to reshedual our family lunch. ____________

We watched a preveiw of the movie before it opened in cinemas. ____________

Challenge words

6 Write the word.

reintroduce ____________

reassess ____________

decelerate ____________

reimburse ____________

precondition ____________

redistribute ____________

depopulate ____________

prerequisite ____________

predetermine ____________

prefabricated ____________

7 Complete the sentence.

The government will ____________ the area to avoid overcrowding.

We had to ____________ the chocolates to make it even.

Being able to swim is a ____________ for scuba diving classes.

He had to ____________ himself, as they did not remember him.

8 Another way to say it. Which challenge word could replace the underlined words?

I promised to <u>repay</u> him for the cost of the pizza. ____________

They plan to <u>review</u> the way students are being taught. ____________

They are going to <u>bring back</u> trams in some cities. ____________

Without that <u>requirement</u>, the match won't go ahead! ____________

All cars have to <u>slow down</u> when they approach the narrow bridge. ____________

List **1 Write the word.**

reliance ______
insurance ______
maintenance ______
guidance ______
clearance ______
residence ______
insistence ______
attendance ______
competence ______
remembrance ______
adolescence ______
significance ______
grievance ______
consequence ______
indulgence ______
prominence ______
disturbance ______
resemblance ______
diligence ______
disappearance ______

2 In a group. Write the list word that belongs in each group.

advice, counsel, ______
ability, capability, ______
youth, teenager, ______
interruption, annoyance, ______
result, outcome, ______
similarity, likeness, ______
house, home, ______

3 Chunks. Rearrange the chunks to make a list word.

nif ca i sig nce ______
br ce an mem re ______
te in ma nan ce ______
ba tur nce dis ______
pe te ce n com ______
dul nce in ge ______
nce en att da ______
bl re an sem ce ______
que con nce se ______

4 Meaning. Which list word means?

Something of great value or importance. ______
The act of being present at an event. ______
That which follows as a result of one's actions. ______
Advice given to help another with a problem or difficulty. ______
The period in which a child develops into an adult. ______
The way in which two or more things are alike. ______
A person's home. ______
A complaint caused by injustice. ______

ance, ence

5 Underline the spelling mistakes. Write the word correctly.

The meintenence of the garden is the gardener's responsibility. ______

The singer quickly rose to prominenance. ______

When I bought my new car, I had to get insurence. ______

The police were called to investigate the disturbence. ______

The family heirloom holds great significence for us. ______

The police are still investigating the man's disappearence. ______

There is just enough clearence for the truck to pass under the bridge. ______

Challenge words

6 Write the word.

resilience ______

turbulence ______

coherence ______

impertinence ______

preference ______

sustenance ______

hindrance ______

insolence ______

acquaintance ______

correspondence ______

7 Hidden words. Find the challenge word.

resiresilienceencme ______

edhuimpertinencesds ______

sgssustenancecesst ______

sdgspreferencedgfsd ______

dgsdinsolencesdfen ______

enceturbulenceturer ______

enercoherencecheo ______

aceacquaintanceauq ______

randhindrancehhin ______

dcecorrespondencecc ______

8 Word clues. Which challenge word matches?

strong movement of air or water ______

something that slows progress ______

rude behaviour ______

someone you have met but don't know well ______

food that maintains life ______

the writing of letters ______

something that is liked better ______

cc, xc

List

raccoon
occupied
exciting
accolade
exceeding
accurate
occupation
exception
excavator
accordance
excise
accede
accumulate
vaccine
access
exclusive
accusation
accustom
exclusion
accrue

1 Write the word.

2 Missing letters. Write the missing letters.

____ding	____ine
____ance	____ise
____late	____pied
____ator	____ess
____oon	____stom
____sive	____sion
____rate	____rue
____ede	____ption

3 Chunks. Rearrange the chunks to make a list word.

a ede cc ____
sive ex clu ____
ade acc ol ____
ci ex se ____
sa accu tion ____
cc va ine ____
tom cus ac ____
late ac mu cu ____

4 Word clues. Which list word matches?

to agree or consent ____
a person's job ____
used to fight disease ____
a small animal ____
something left out or different ____
to remove or cut out ____
able to thrill ____
praise for an achievement ____

5 Underline the spelling mistakes. Write the word correctly.

Jack's excluesion from the team was unexpected. ______
The racone is a native North American mammal. ______
To see the famous actress, we needed a special acess pass. ______
The driver was given a ticket for exceding the speed limit. ______
They were too ocupied to notice her arrival. ______
A vacsine helps to protect the body against a disease. ______
If I keep putting money in my bank account, it will acrue a lot of interest. ______

Challenge words

6 Write the word.

vaccination ______
succumb ______
succinct ______
acclimatise ______
exculpate ______
accentuate ______
successor ______
impeccable ______
acceleration ______
exclamatory ______

7 Hidden words. Find the challenge word.

dfgdfsuccumbdfd ______
sgsexculpatesdgs ______
sdfsimpeccabledfssd ______
dfsdgaccelerationsds ______
sdfssuccinctgs ______
sfeaccentuategvvcx ______
susiesuccessorsdnsii ______
astisacclimatisecclim ______
atiovaccinationcavv ______
toryexclamatoryclae ______

8 Word clues. Which challenge word matches?

to free from guilt or blame ______
a person that comes after ______
flawless or perfect ______
to adapt ______
to give more emphasis ______

Tricky words

List **1 Write the word.**

buys ____________
built ____________
beauty ____________
awhile ____________
believe ____________
tomorrow ____________
doctor ____________
caught ____________
hospital ____________
brought ____________
wouldn't ____________
definitely ____________
enough ____________
rhythm ____________
dangerous ____________
average ____________
sincerely ____________
suppose ____________
probably ____________
stationery ____________

2 Name.

EMERGENCY

3 Missing syllable. Write the missing syllable.

av ________ age
________ lieve
e ________
sta ________ ery
beau ________
defi ________ ly
________ morrow
________ cerely
hospi ________
________ pose

4 Word clues. Which list word matches?

the day after today ____________
where sick people find care ____________
not safe ____________
regular repetition of sound ____________
writing materials ____________
a person trained to care for the sick ____________
for a short time ____________
genuinely, truly ____________

Tricky words

5 Complete each sentence with a list word.

After they removed my appendix, I stayed overnight in the ______________.

Tran ______________ a large tower out of blocks.

The ______________ listened to my heartbeat with a stethoscope.

I knew I ______________ be able to run at the carnival as I had broken my leg.

Driving too fast is very ______________.

I was ______________ sorry for accidentally knocking my brother over.

I like that song because it has a good ______________.

Challenge words

6 Write the word.

tongue ______________

satellite ______________

embarrass ______________

separate ______________

appreciate ______________

fatigue ______________

appropriate ______________

existence ______________

experience ______________

suspicious ______________

7 Word clues. Which challenge word matches?

to set apart ______________

the organ in your mouth ______________

being tired in your body or mind ______________

to cause someone to feel awkward ______________

being cautious of someone or something ______________

something that orbits the earth or another planet ______________

8 Another way to say it. Which list word could replace the underlined word?

I did not mean to <u>humiliate</u> him in front of his friends. ______________

I felt great <u>exhaustion</u> after running the marathon. ______________

Dad had to <u>part</u> the two squabbling children. ______________

We had to wear <u>suitable</u> clothes to the wedding. ______________

Abseiling at camp was a great <u>adventure</u>. ______________

I was <u>distrustful</u> of his behaviour. ______________

Suffix: ness

List

laziness
toughness
quietness
uneasiness
liveliness
suddenness
wholeness
narrowness
remoteness
strangeness
numbness
idleness
weariness
lawlessness
robustness
drowsiness
ruthlessness
homelessness
vagueness
stubbornness

1 Write the word.

2 Missing letters. Write the missing letters.

na________
su________
law________
laz________
li________
v________
id________
stu________
re________
we________

3 Unscramble the list words.

ssnsseeelomh
ssssneellwa
bsuntsseor
leessnhow
airensswe
aisnssenue
inwssesdor
sssseelnthur

4 In a group. Write the list word that belongs in each group.

abruptness, quickness,
weirdness, oddness,
tiredness, sleepiness,
coldness, deadness,
silence, noiselessness,
thinness, tightness,
cruelty, heartlessness,
sturdiness, firmness,

Suffix: ness

5 Underline the spelling mistakes. Write the word correctly.

The little girl's stubbornesse caused the delay. __________
The suddeness of the storm meant that we got very wet. __________
Due to my lasiness, my room is still a mess. __________
The kwietness of the library made it pleasant to work in. __________
Homelisnes amongst the elderly is on the increase. __________
He felt a growing sense of uneaseness. __________
I went to bed as drosiness overcame me. __________
The numbness in my toes is due to the icy weather. __________

Challenge words

6 Write the word.

assertiveness __________
expressiveness __________
attractiveness __________
competitiveness __________
righteousness __________
inventiveness __________
effectiveness __________
unpleasantness __________
appropriateness __________
uniqueness __________

7 Hidden words. Find the challenge word.

hugassertivenessdf __________
buattractivenessdv __________
fcompetitivenesssd __________
hduinventivenessd __________
dfeseffectivenesssd __________
fsesuniquenessvsds __________
essunpleasantnessu __________
nesrighteousnessrig __________

8 Word clues. Which challenge word matches?

being forward and aggressive __________
morally correct __________
a strong desire to win __________
thinking up good ideas __________
different from everything else __________

Irregular plurals

List

data
strata
series
crises
pliers
media
offspring
fishermen
tweezers
sportsmen
larvae
species
bacteria
barracks
crossroads
runners-up
salespeople
policewomen
teaspoonsful
mothers-in-law

1 Write the word.

2 Name.

3 Chunks. Rearrange the syllables to make a list word.

ses cri
spoons tea ful
er fish men
di me a
racks bar
peo ple sales
ta stra
vae lar
orts men sp
lice men po wo

4 Meaning. Which list word means?

Layers of rock in the earth's surface.
Metal tools, with two arms, used for plucking hairs.
The children or young of a particular human or animal.
Microscopic organisms that cause living things to decay.
Buildings or groups of buildings used to house soldiers.
The place where two roads meet or intersect.
Insects after they have hatched, but before they become adults.

Irregular plurals

5 Complete each sentence with a list word.

We collected ______________ from many different sources.

We used social ______________ to help promote our school's fundraiser.

There are many different ______________ of dogs.

We slowed down as we approached the ______________ to avoid an accident.

When Banjo got caught in the wire fence, we used two pairs of ______________ to cut him free.

After training the soldiers were sent back to their ______________ .

Challenge words

6 Write the word.

criteria ______________

analyses ______________

diagnoses ______________

vertebrae ______________

personnel ______________

phenomena ______________

culs-de-sac ______________

parentheses ______________

memorabilia ______________

headquarters ______________

7 Word clues. Which challenge word matches?

bones forming the spinal column ______________

objects with sentimental value ______________

the main offices of an organisation ______________

identification of illnesses ______________

people employed by an organisation ______________

the standards by which something is judged ______________

8 Complete each sentence.

The ______________ were all evacuated when the building caught fire.

The physiotherapist popped her ______________ back into alignment.

My uncle has lots of football ______________ in his garage.

The spy reported back to ______________ after every mission.

I placed the extra information in the sentence inside ______________ .

ion, ian

List

1 Write the word.

mansion ____________
edition ____________
foundation ____________
revision ____________
conclusion ____________
attention ____________
invitation ____________
electrician ____________
conversion ____________
supervision ____________
sensation ____________
impression ____________
inclusion ____________
repetition ____________
preparation ____________
seclusion ____________
exhibition ____________
suggestion ____________
collision ____________
comprehension ____________

2 Name.

You're invited to my
BIRDTHDAY
– PARTY –
5

3 Missing letters. Write the missing letters.

edi________	conve________
at________ion	concl________
sug________	fou________
inv________	com________
sec________	exhi________
ma________	repe________
col________	impr________
prep________	sup________
incl________	elec________
sens________	revi________

4 Word clues. Which list word matches?

understanding ____________
a very large house ____________
an initial perception ____________
a person who rewires lights ____________
over and over and over ____________
the base of something ____________
going over something you have learnt before ____________
the process of changing ____________

5 Underline the spelling mistakes. Write the word correctly.

I received the invitatian to her party in the mail. ____________

This editian of the magazine is not as good as the last one. ____________

I was upset that no one took my suggestian seriously. ____________

He did not make a very good first impressian. ____________

We bought our tickets to the exhibitian online. ____________

Two cars on the highway had a terrible colision. ____________

A lot of preparatian went into getting everything ready for the party. ____________

Challenge words

6 Write the word.

transfusion ____________

succession ____________

concentration ____________

percussion ____________

identification ____________

paediatrician ____________

recommendation ____________

accommodation ____________

aggression ____________

diagnostician ____________

7 Word clues. Which challenge word matches?

children's doctor ____________

the transfer of blood ____________

drums and cymbals ____________

to think hard; focus ____________

a suggestion or proposal ____________

a place where someone may stay ____________

a document that tells who you are ____________

someone who finds the cause of an illness ____________

8 Complete each sentence.

The mother is taking her children to see the ____________.

To get on the plane, we had to present some ____________.

The doctor advised us that a blood ____________ wasn't necessary.

He plays a ____________ instrument in the school band.

The three explosions came in quick ____________.

Eponyms

List

August
valentine
titanic
lynch
Friday
flora
fauna
bedlam
leotard
jovial
Celsius
galvanise
tawdry
spartan
paisley
derrick
tantalise
meander
marathon
raglan

1 Write the word.

____

2 Name.

3 Missing letters. Write the missing letters.

spa__________
ga__________
va__________
flo__________
Fr__________
pai__________
tan__________
mar__________
bed__________
me__________
ly__________

4 Word clues. Which list word matches?

plants __________
animals __________
garment worn by dancers or gymnasts __________
intricate design of curly shapes __________
a scene of confusion __________
cheap and showy __________
a machine made to lift heavy loads __________
a temperature scale __________

Eponyms

5 Complete each sentence with a list word.

The ________________ explosion destroyed many villages.
He tried to ________________ me by slowly unwrapping the chocolate.
The ________________ in the meadow blooms in spring.
Crocodiles, kangaroos and koalas are just some of the ________________ found in Australia.
Jane packed her ________________ and tights before going to ballet.
Water will boil at 100 degrees ________________.
The athlete was training hard for his 42 km ________________.

Challenge words

6 Write the word.

nemesis ________________
spoonerism ________________
stoicism ________________
stentorian ________________
mausoleum ________________
saturnine ________________
odyssey ________________
malapropism ________________
gargantuan ________________
narcissist ________________

7 Hidden words. Find the challenge word.

ssdydodysseydfsdf ________________
dfgdnarcissistdfevs ________________
fssdfspoonerismsde ________________
sdfsgargantuanfsds ________________
lepmausoleummau ________________
ssienemesisnem ________________
simostoicismstoic ________________
ninesaturninesture ________________
simmalapropismpo ________________

8 Word clues. Which challenge word matches?

switching the initial sounds of one or more words ________________
a humorous misuse of a word ________________
a large tomb ________________
a rival or arch enemy ________________
huge, gigantic ________________
someone who loves themself ________________

Vowel exceptions

List

1 Write the word.

double ____________
ahead ____________
ocean ____________
breath ____________
deaden ____________
heading ____________
healthy ____________
aunt ____________
certain ____________
cereal ____________
dreadful ____________
feather ____________
measure ____________
bargain ____________
curtain ____________
certainly ____________
cleanser ____________
villain ____________
captain ____________
fountain ____________

2 Name.

3 Unscramble these list words.

ylniatrec ____________
dnaeed ____________
acntrie ____________
lufdaerd ____________
ngbaira ____________
edhaa ____________
ubodle ____________
threaef ____________
anerselc ____________
niatnuof ____________

4 Meaning. Which list word means?

Twice the amount or number of something. ____________
A thing bought or offered at a cheaper price. ____________
A piece of material hung from a window to block out light. ____________
To make something less intense. ____________
Something terrible, causing or involving great fear. ____________
Known to be true; without any doubt. ____________
The air you take into your lungs and let out. ____________
A large expanse of water covering three quarters of the earth's surface.
____

Vowel exceptions

5 Complete each sentence with a list word.

If you ________________ ten, you get twenty.

I threw coins into the ________________ and made a wish.

The ________________ was working on his evil plan to defeat the superhero.

Sunlight streamed through the crack in my ________________ and woke me up.

We all ran from the ________________ at the sound of a shark alarm.

We had to ________________ our new fridge, to make sure it would fit in the kitchen.

The ________________ of the ship got his crew back to shore safely.

Challenge words

6 Write the word.

breadth ________________

coupon ________________

gauge ________________

caustic ________________

mauve ________________

Bedouin ________________

pageant ________________

journal ________________

hydraulic ________________

cauliflower ________________

7 Word clues. Which challenge word matches?

to estimate ________________

operated by water ________________

something you write in ________________

able to burn or corrode ________________

nomadic people of the desert ________________

a public show about historical events ________________

the measured distance from one side to another ________________

8 Complete each sentence.

We used a tape measure to measure the ________________ of the new cabinet.

A ________________ is a vegetable with a large white head made up of firm flowers.

I try to write in my ________________ every night.

I was trying hopelessly to ________________ his reaction to the news.

I decided to paint my nails a deep ________________ colour.

Plurals

6.30

List

1 Write the word.

surveys ______

jerseys ______

seventies ______

victories ______

emergencies ______

castaways ______

medleys ______

galaxies ______

boundaries ______

balconies ______

authorities ______

societies ______

allergies ______

corduroys ______

burglaries ______

amenities ______

luxuries ______

currencies ______

enquiries ______

apologies ______

2 Complete the table.

allergy	allergies
apology	
galaxy	
luxury	
victory	
boundary	
enquiry	
society	

3 Missing letters. Write the missing letters.

su _ v _ ys	se _ _ _ ti _ _
_ oun _ ar _ es	_ ast _ _ _ y _
c _ rd _ r _ _ s	_ alc _ _ i _ _
_ ux _ ri _ s	bur _ _ ar _ _ _
m _ dl _ ys	all _ _ g _ _ _
_ oci _ t _ _ s	en _ _ _ ri _ _
v _ ct _ r _ _ s	_ polo _ _ _ _
_ ut _ ori _ _ es	gal _ _ i _ _

4 Word clues. Which list word matches?

worn by people who play sport ______

collections of stars and matter held together by gravity ______

people who have been shipwrecked ______

things that make a place more convenient or pleasing ______

money used in different countries ______

reactions to certain foods ______

people who have the right to give orders ______

platforms that extend from the outside of buildings ______

Plurals

5 Complete each sentence with a list word.

Both of my grandparents are in their ________________.

I have ________________ to pollen and nuts.

My uncle and aunt sent their ________________ as they couldn't come to my party.

The ________________ built a shelter from tree branches on the small island.

We were careful to lock our doors as there have been a lot of ________________.

The police use a siren when they are on their way to ________________.

The business received many ________________ after their advertisement was shown.

The universe is made up of many ________________.

Challenge words

6 Write the word.

impurities ________________

secretaries ________________

disabilities ________________

uncertainties ________________

commentaries ________________

symphonies ________________

controversies ________________

nationalities ________________

accessories ________________

technologies ________________

7 Hidden words. Find the challenge word.

divsdfimpuritiesvfsed ________________

shfucontroversiessesve ________________

fgvsevcaccessoriesdves ________________

scgvscommentariescvf ________________

sfsesesecretariesxvsr ________________

feedisabilitiesvsdgvde ________________

logistechnologiestench ________________

litisnationalitiesnagtis ________________

poshsymphoniesisien ________________

certuncertaintiesitsse ________________

8 Complete each sentence.

Although their ________________ make life difficult, they always have a smile on their faces.

She wasn't sure which ________________ to wear with her new outfit.

Travelling the world means you meet people of different ________________.

Dad likes to listen to sport ________________on the radio.

Suffix: ly

List

1 Write the word.

heavily ____________________
lawfully ____________________
blissfully ____________________
suddenly ____________________
regularly ____________________
remarkably ____________________
clumsily ____________________
cheekily ____________________
brutally ____________________
frequently ____________________
absolutely ____________________
annually ____________________
typically ____________________
boastfully ____________________
brilliantly ____________________
separately ____________________
curiously ____________________
casually ____________________
unfortunately ____________________
ashamedly ____________________

2 Word building. Add suffixes to build words.

sudden	suddenly
cheeky	
clumsy	
brilliant	
heavy	
annual	
absolute	
regular	

3 Missing letters. Write the missing letters.

che____________ hea____________
boa____________ ann____________
ash____________ brill____________
abs____________ reg____________
bru____________ sud____________
typ____________ law____________
blis____________ fre____________
curi____________ unf____________

4 Chunks. Rearrange the letters to make a list word.

mar ly kab re ____________
en dd ly su ____________
que nt ly fre ____________
pi cal ly ty ____________
so lut ab ely ____________
a ra t ely sep ____________
ham ed as ly ____________
for tun ely at un ____________
iou sly cur ____________
ful ast bo ly ____________
ian brill tly ____________
tal bru ly ____________
nu al an ly ____________
ki ly ee ch ____________
lar u reg ly ____________
ful iss ly bl ____________

5 Underline the spelling mistakes. Write the word correctly.

She strolled casuely in the park on the warm summer's day. ______

My baby brother chekely ran away from our dad. ______

The diamond shone briliantely in the sunshine. ______

I like to exercise regulely to stay fit and healthy. ______

We meet anualy for a family reunion. ______

Ken frequentely went to the library to borrow books. ______

I sudenley remembered that I had soccer training and ran down to the field. ______

Challenge words

6 Write the word.

traditionally ______

anxiously ______

accidentally ______

academically ______

artificially ______

consequently ______

competently ______

undoubtedly ______

aggressively ______

alternatively ______

7 Hidden words. Find the challenge word.

ahdiacademicallydgm ______

djhxcompetentlyxgvf ______

sdndundoubtedlyfvd ______

gddtraditionallyvbdb ______

dlgsaccidentallyxbll ______

vsdartificiallyvsdsrsd ______

aasiugalternativelyss ______

sdudaggressivelydvhd ______

saopconsequentlysfes ______

skoskanxiouslyfevxc ______

8 Another way to say it. Which challenge word could replace the underlined word?

I waited <u>nervously</u> for the doctor to tell me my results. ______

The red stone in her ring was <u>synthetically</u> produced. ______

I didn't get much sleep last night and <u>therefore</u> was very sleepy today. ______

He was sent to the principal after he <u>forcefully</u> pushed his classmate. ______

Suffix: ity

List | **1 Write the word.**

authority ______
hospitality ______
availability ______
nationality ______
liability ______
capacity ______
originality ______
suitability ______
respectability ______
technicality ______
reliability ______
sustainability ______
peculiarity ______
authenticity ______
irregularity ______
superiority ______
profitability ______
compatibility ______
individuality ______
anonymity ______

2 Missing letters. Write the missing letters.

a _ t _ ori _ y
pr _ _ ita _ _ l _ ty
_ iab _ li _ y
su _ t _ bi _ ity
su _ er _ ori _ y
_ es _ ecta _ il _ ty
r _ l _ abi _ ity
pe _ ul _ ar _ _ _

3 Chunks. Rearrange the syllables to make a list word.

bil ta spec ity re ______
a bil ity vail a ______
ni ch cal te ity ______
tain a bil ity sus ______
fit a ity bil pro ______
pat bil ity i com ______
rreg la rity i u ______
then ci ty au ti ______

4 Meaning. Which list word means?

The state of remaining unknown. ______
The quality of being true or genuine. ______
Something strange or odd. ______
The state of being better than others. ______
The friendly and generous treatment of guests, visitors and strangers. ______
The right or power to give orders, make decisions and control people. ______

5 Underline the spelling mistakes. Write the word correctly.

Phoebe liked to express her individooality through her poetry. ______

My grandparents, nationalitee is Japanese. ______

Harry won an award for the originately of his project. ______

My new phone and computer lack compatibelity. ______

The school's debating team won on a technikality. ______

We have to protect the environment to ensure its sustaneability. ______

We received a certificate of orthenticiy with the designer necklace. ______

The news program blurred the man's face to ensure his annonnimity. ______

Challenge words

6 Write the word.

vulnerability ______

feasibility ______

eccentricity ______

tranquillity ______

spontaneity ______

inevitability ______

accessibility ______

municipality ______

susceptibility ______

confidentiality ______

7 Word clues. Which challenge word matches?

calm, peace, serenity ______

oddness or peculiarity ______

certainty ______

practicality ______

a secret ______

a town's local government ______

acting on the spur of the moment ______

a state of being easily hurt ______

8 Another way to say it. Which challenge word could replace the underlined word?

It was her <u>oddness</u> that made her stand out from the crowd. ______

The <u>secrecy</u> of the project meant that I couldn't tell anyone. ______

She often visited the lake because of its <u>peacefulness</u>. ______

The <u>convenience</u> of the corner store is what makes it so popular. ______

ary, ery, ory

List

1 Write the word.

List	Write the word
literary	
January	
bribery	
cannery	
livery	
trickery	
planetary	
legendary	
imaginary	
sensory	
customary	
advisory	
artillery	
centenary	
accessory	
adversary	
compulsory	
supervisory	
documentary	
complimentary	

2 Word clues. Which list word matches?

assisting a criminal ______

opponent or enemy ______

large weapons ______

having to do with our senses ______

comes before February ______

existing only in your mind ______

3 Chunks. Rearrange the syllables to make a list word.

til y ler ar ______

y ar er lit ______

y ad vis or ______

y u Jan ar ______

ry so vi per su ______

liv y er ______

so com ry pul ______

y plan tar e ______

4 Sort the words.

ery	ary	ory

5 Complete each sentence with a list word.

They gave him a reduced sentence as he was only an a__________ to the crime.

The teacher only had c__________ things to say about her class.

A c__________ marks the hundredth anniversary of an event.

It is c__________ for the bride to wear white on her wedding day.

For our group project, we are making a d__________ about the history of our school.

There was a mix up at the c__________ and dog food was put in baked beans tins!

Challenge words

6 Write the word.

contemporary __________

parliamentary __________

subsidiary __________

beneficiary __________

sedentary __________

contradictory __________

conciliatory __________

chicanery __________

auxiliary __________

supplementary __________

7 Word clues. Which challenge word matches?

the clever use of deception __________

related to the subject but less important __________

involving little physical activity __________

extra support __________

one who will receive or inherit certain benefits __________

belonging to the present time __________

8 Complete each sentence.

The crew started to worry when their a__________ power shut off.

The teacher uses s__________ materials to help educate her students.

We were told to focus on the main point, disregarding all s__________ information.

My mother is the b__________ of my grandfather's will.

They told c__________ stories about what really happened.

ably, ibly

List **1 Write the word.**

suitably ______
notably ______
reliably ______
remarkably ______
fashionably ______
sociably ______
responsibly ______
comfortably ______
probably ______
reasonably ______
preferably ______
miserably ______
considerably ______
forcibly ______
noticeably ______
arguably ______
predictably ______
incredibly ______
impossibly ______
presumably ______

2 Word building. Add suffixes to build words.

reasonable	reasonably
arguable	
miserable	
suitable	
impossible	
preferable	
fashionable	
notable	

3 Unscramble these list words.

psyilbmsio ______
ylbakarmer ______
ulsytbia ______
iysbolac ______
tynbola ______
bpybalor ______
eefrbaylrp ______
yblicrof ______

4 Chunks. Rearrange the syllables to make a list word.

su ma pre bly ______
ta dic bly pre ______
cre bly di in ______
a fer bly pre ______
sid a er bly con ______
for ta com bly ______
spon bly re si ______
mar bly ka re ______

ion bly a fash ______
tice a no bly ______
er bly mis a ______
son bly a rea ______
pos bly im si ______
gu bly ar a ______
ci bly for ______
bly ba pro ______

5 Underline the spelling mistakes. Write the word correctly.

The pizza was argueably the best I had ever eaten! ______

Zachery has grown noticably taller in the last year. ______

Tina sat comfortablie in the armchair and read a book. ______

The boys were fashionabely dressed for the party. ______

They are running late; presummably because of the traffic. ______

The police officer had to forcibely remove the criminal from the car. ______

Challenge words

6 Write the word.

inseparably ______
unquestionably ______
unbelievably ______
undeniably ______
understandably ______
immeasurably ______
imperceptibly ______
incomprehensibly ______
uncontrollably ______
impeccably ______

7 Hidden words. Find the challenge word.

gdfunderstandablyfg ______
dfgimpeccablydfeef ______
fgdincomprehensiblym ______
dufundeniablyfgfdn ______
gqunquestionablygy ______
dfgimmeasurablydfg ______
fgimperceptiblygdfpe ______
ablyinseparablyinsep ______
llysunbelievablylievb ______
rolluncontrollablyollr ______

8 Another way to say it. Which list word could replace the underlined word?

The sun <u>gradually</u> sank below the horizon. ______

She is always <u>perfectly</u> dressed. ______

The evidence showed that it was <u>irrefutably</u> a case of mistaken identity. ______

He was <u>justifiably</u> upset when he heard the news about his grandfather. ______

I found her laughing <u>hysterically</u> and couldn't help but laugh too. ______

in, im, ir, il

List

1 Write the word.

improper ____________
impersonal ____________
inability ____________
injustice ____________
indistinct ____________
immovable ____________
impossible ____________
incapable ____________
inconsistent ____________
independent ____________
illicit ____________
irrational ____________
immaturity ____________
inadequate ____________
irregularly ____________
impatience ____________
indecisive ____________
irresistible ____________
inconvenient ____________
inconsiderate ____________

2 Word clues. Which list word matches?

without reason or sense ____________
free, not ruled by another ____________
not able to happen ____________
not thinking of another ____________
impossible to resist ____________
not clearly defined ____________
not permitted by law ____________
not following a pattern ____________

3 Missing letters. Write the missing letters.

ir _ eg _ lar _ y
_ n _ ust _ _ e
i _ conv _ ni _ nt
in _ ap _ _ le
i _ m _ tur _ _ y
_ _ dep _ nde _ t
_ _ ad_ _ ua _ _
_ _ pati _ _ _ _
_ _ consid _ _ _ _ _

4 Sort the words.

in	im	ir	il

in, im, ir, il

5 Underline the spelling mistakes. Write the word correctly.

It is illegal to buy, sell or use ellicit items. ____________

My impateince grew the naughtier the children became. ____________

Without my glasses, all I could see were indistincte shapes. ____________

He failed because of his inadeqwate preparation. ____________

His school attendance has been very inconsestent this year. ____________

He got into trouble for his enconsiderate behaviour. ____________

She did not like camping because of her irrationel fear of wombats.

____

Her indesisiv nature makes it difficult for her to choose something.

____

Challenge words

6 Write the word.

irreversible ____________

incompatible ____________

imperceptible ____________

indestructible ____________

inefficient ____________

inoffensive ____________

inappropriate ____________

inconceivable ____________

inconspicuous ____________

indistinguishable ____________

7 Word clues. Which challenge word matches?

not able to be damaged or broken

____

not likely to be noticed or seen

____

not right for the time or place

____

impossible to imagine or understand

____

impossible to tell the difference

____

impossible to change ____________

8 Complete each sentence.

His comments were ____________ and didn't upset anyone.

I groaned as I thought of the ____________ damage I had caused.

My laptop and new USB were ____________, so I had to reformat them.

When wearing the same clothes, the twins were ____________ from each other.

ancy, ency

List

agency
decency
fluency
emergency
vacancy
infancy
urgency
frequency
hesitancy
presidency
accountancy
competency
excellency
truancy
dependency
consistency
consultancy
leniency
occupancy
despondency

1 Write the word.

2 Sort the words.

ancy	ency

3 Chunks. Rearrange the chunks to make a list word.

den si cy pre ______
pe cy ten com ______
oun cy tan acc ______
sis ten con cy ______
pen cy den de ______

3 Word clues. Which list word matches?

an unfilled space ______
very early childhood ______
a serious situation that calls for quick action ______
feeling doubt or uncertainty ______
the number of times an event happens ______
not strict with rules ______
hopelessness ______
being away from school without permission ______

ancy, ency

5 Complete each sentence with a list word.

There was a ________________ at the hotel, so we booked in for the night.

I could hear the ________________ in his voice and knew that the matter was serious.

Judges in court are often referred to as "Your ________________".

My older cousin is studying ________________ at university.

The ________________ of earthquakes in our area has risen in the last year.

Rochelle was going to run for the class ________________.

Challenge words

6 Write the word.

transparency ________________

buoyancy ________________

deficiency ________________

expediency ________________

proficiency ________________

coherency ________________

efficiency ________________

complacency ________________

absorbency ________________

ascendancy ________________

7 Word clues. Which challenge word matches?

the quick performance of a task ________________

being easy to understand ________________

being able to soak up moisture ________________

being able to see through ________________

satisfaction with one's situation ________________

able to float ________________

8 Complete each sentence.

She had to take special tablets to supplement her calcium ________________.

Our ________________ allows us to float in water.

Luke's ________________ at completing his homework meant he had more time to play outside.

When it comes to playing video games, he has a high level of ________________.

After playing badly in the first half, they once again gained the ________________ in the second half.

RULES AND GENERALISATIONS

Prefixes

in, im, ir, il — The prefix *in* turns a word into its opposite, accurate → *inaccurate*. If a word starts with *b*, *m* or *p*, use *im*, practical → *impractical*. If a word starts with *r*, use *ir*, relevant → *irrelevant*. If a word starts with *l*, use *il*, like legal → *illegal*.

re, de, pre — The prefix *re* can mean to go back or to do again, locate → *relocate*. The prefix *de* means to remove, mobilise → *demobilise*. The prefix *pre* means before, mature → *premature*.

un, dis, mis — The prefix *un*, *dis* or *mis* turns a word into its opposite. wise → *unwise* satisfied → *dissatisfied* fortune → *misfortune*

Suffixes

ly — If an adjective ends in *consonant* + *y*, change the *y* to *i* then add *ly*, cheeky → *cheekily*. If the adjective ends in *ic*, add *ally*, academic → *academically*.

ion, ian — Turn some verbs that end in *t*, *te*, *s*, *se*, *d* or *de* into nouns by adding *ion*. attract → *attraction* communicate → *communication* collide → *collision* Turn some words that end in *c* or *cs* into nouns by adding *ian*, politics → *politician*.

able, ible — If the base word ends in *e*, drop the *e* before adding *able*, admire → *admirable*. If the base word ends in *consonant* + *y*, change the *y* to *i* before adding *able*, envy → *enviable*. Some adjectives take the suffix *ible*, terror → *terrible*.

ably, ibly — Turn adjectives that end in *able* and *ible* into adverbs by dropping the *e* and adding *y*, reasonable → *reasonably* or incredibly → *incredibly*.

ness — Adding the suffix *ness* to an adjective turns it into a noun, narrow → *narrowness*. If the adjective ends in *y*, change it to *i* before adding *ness*, lively → *liveliness*.

ity — Turn some words into nouns by adding the *ity*, equal → *equality*. If a word ends in *e*, drop the *e* before adding *ity*, opportune → *opportunity*. If a word ends in *le*, change *le* to *il* before adding *ity*, stable → *stability*.

ic — Turn some words into adjectives by adding *ic*, art → *artistic*.

ence, ance — Turn some verbs into nouns by adding *ance*, annoy → *annoyance*. Turn adjectives that end in *ant* into nouns by changing *ant* to *ance*, fragrant → *fragrance*. Turn some verbs into nouns by adding *ence*, emerge → *emergence*. Turn adjectives that end in *ent* into nouns by changing *ent* to *ence*, violent → *violence*.

ancy, ency — Turn adjectives that end in *ant* and *ent* into nouns by replacing *ant* and *ent* with *ancy* and *ency*, extravagant → *extravagancy*; urgent → *urgency*. Turn common nouns that end in *ant* or *ent* into abstract nouns by replacing *ant* and *ent* with *ancy* and *ency*, like infant → *infancy* and agent → *agency*.

ous — If the base word ends in *e*, drop the *e* before adding *ous*, ridicule → *ridiculous*. If the base word ends in *consonant* + *y*, change the *y* to *i* then add *ous*, glory → *glorious*.

ist — When *ist* is added to a word, it shows someone who does something, cartoon → *cartoonist*. Sometimes we drop the last letters before adding *ist*, like piano → *pianist*.